MW01067363

SECRET MAGIC SPELLS & CURSES

OF THE ANCIENT ROMANY GYPSIES

Vadoma Waylan

SECRET MAGIC SPELLS & CURSES

OF THE ANCIENT ROMANY GYPSIES

Gypsy Spells and Incantations

Romani mythology is the myth, folklore, religion, traditions, and legends of the Romani people. (The Romani are sometimes referred to as Gypsies, though many consider this a slur. The Romani are a nomadic culture which is thought to have originated in India during the Middle Ages. They migrated widely, particularly to Europe. Some legends (particularly from non-Romani peoples) say that certain Romani have passive psychic powers such as empathy, precognition, retrocognition, or psychometry. Other legends include the ability to levitate, travel through astral projection by way of meditation, invoke curses or blessings, conjure or channel spirits, and skill with illusion-casting.

The gypsy people are wanderers. Their ancestors are thought to have come from India around A.D. 1300. They wandered through Iran to Armenia, Syria, Egypt, and North Africa.

They then moved into Hungary, Romania, France, Russia, and even England. It is the ones from Romania that we will deal with.

These people were nomadic, and very few settled down and established homes. They were called by various names such as Children of Little Egypt, Tziganes, Maniches, and Romanies.

Gypsies have always jealously guarded their customs and traditions, so much of their magical practices are not known. But the spells and incantations that are known have proved to be very powerful.

Hitler was a black magician and feared anyone who like himself had any esoteric or occult knowledge, either good or bad. He would kill anyone that he suspected of having occult links. For this reason, thousands of gypsies in World War II were slaughtered by Hitler, and his Nazi concentration camps housed many of them.

Gypsies are always thought of as pranksters and petty thieves. This is to a certain extent still the case today. Although it is commonly believed to be true, it is a misconception. The Romany people were skilled musicians and metalworkers, since ancient times they have been blacksmiths and horse traders.

They were also skilled and experienced in the art of magic. In this book we have given several powerful spells and incantations. If they are used in conjunction with the instructions we have given, they will bring you all the love and happiness you deserve.

These spells are very powerful and sacred, they must be treated with respect. If they are used wisely, they will prove to be very effective.

They do not come from the fairground gypsies, who pretend to read your fortune, by making their predictions so wide ranged that at least some of them will fit your circumstances. These fairground gypsies have little to do with the Romany gypsies of which we speak. These fairground gypsies should be avoided.

There is a story of one of these gypsies. The "gypsy" would have a helper stand not too far away from her stall. This helper would watch the people who were about to go into the stall, to see if they would give any clues to their identity. He would watch the people take off their wedding rings and go into the gypsy's stall. Then he would give her a sign telling her what he saw. The "gypsy" would then tell the person that they were married. This would leave the client in awe and ensure that he would believe the rest of her predictions.

It should be noted that with the incantations that follow, the pronunciation should be as if you were speaking French. This seems to give the most efficient results. The language is based on the ancient Sanskrit or Prakrit. These spells are very old and very powerful. They can work wonders in your life, if only you let them.

(If you have any difficulty in pronouncing the words you can instead write them on - preferably parchment-paper - with a black pen all the while thinking of your desire as you do so. Whether spoken or written these incantations will work).

Powerful Love Spells

As with all these spells, it is advisable to sit down, for a few moments, and think about the reasons behind your desire. There are three things to consider:

1. Do you really want this thing?

2. Will what you want be good for you?

3. Is it necessary to use a spell to achieve your aims?

After you have considered your options and have decided to go ahead with your objective, you must choose the appropriate spell.

The spell that most suits you only you will know. If one fails, then try another, but the one you feel most comfortable with will generally, be the one for you.

You may wish to use an attraction spell, or you may wish to bind the person whom you seek. Whichever spell you choose keep in mind that you are calling on power that has worked for the Gypsy people for centuries. It will work for you, if you treat the spells with respect and not as a joke or party-piece.

Now that you have considered your options let us begin the spell work.

To attract a female

Obtain a green candle, of any size or shape. Wash this candle under running water and leave to dry. Once the candle has completely dried, inscribe on it the name of the woman/girl you wish to come to you. The inscription can be made with a knife or by heating, slightly, a needle. The name inscribed should be the most used one, that is the name that everyone calls her. For example, her name may be Elizabeth, but everyone calls her Beth, or Liza or Lisa, whatever she is called by the majority of people who know her, this is the name to use.

This candle now represents the woman.

In a passive frame of mind, visualize the woman you desire standing before you. Light the candle. As you hold this picture in your mind state in a loud voice the following incantation three times:

"Me jiuklo, yoy jiukli

Y oy tover, me pori

Me kokosh, yoy catra

Ada ada, me kamav!"

After reciting the above, visualize the woman running with open arms towards you, as you say:

"You want . . . . (state your name) to be your lover".

Repeat this ten times.

The spell is now complete, and you should relax and return to your normal business, in complete knowledge that your spell has worked.

To attract a male

Obtain a green candle. Prepare this in the same way as before by washing it in running water and leaving it to dry. Then on this candle inscribe the name of your lover-to-be. As we mentioned before, this can be done with a knife or by using a warm needle.

Again, in a passive frame of mind, visualize the man you desire standing before you. Feel his presence. No

"Upro p~uv hin but pu~uva

Kas kamav mange th'avla!

Barvol, barvol, salciye,

Briga na hin mange!

Y ov tover, me pori

Yov Kokosh, me catra

Ada, ada me kamav".

These spells will not only make the person attracted to you, but they should also bring them to you. You will probably find that the person will go out of his/her way to be near you. The person may try to seduce you or may not approach you at all. If this happens you must weigh the situation. The person may be too shy to make the first move.

We have found that many students fail in love spells because they refuse to see that the spell has already worked. A spell will make a person attracted to you, but if you do not act on this then nothing may well happen. Don't worry, you will know if the spell has worked, even shy people find it hard to disguise their feelings.

So, if this does happen, it is up to you to approach the person.

Ask them to go for a drink or whatever interests them. You will not regret it!

14

A Gypsy binding spell

This spell, if performed properly, should prove to be very effective. It must be performed while the moon is waning (that state between a new and full moon).

Acquire two white candles, a red or pink candle and a piece of rope, string or thread of the same colour, at least six inches long.

Place all the paraphernalia in a circle of salt, about eight inches in diameter.

One of the white candles will represent you, while the other will represent your prospective lover. These candles should be inscribed with the names of the persons they represent, using a knife or warm needle.

The other candle is symbolic of your objective aim, red for passion, or pink for love, use whichever is appropriate.

These candles should now be consecrated for the work in hand.

Hold each candle in turn, while visualizing your desired outcome, and repeat:

"You are now blessed and clean and free, you will fulfil and bring this wish to me".

Light the objective candle and then lift the two subject candles, one in each hand. Light these two with flame of the objective candle and in a loud commanding voice say:

"Kay o kam, avriavel

Kiya mange lele beshel

Kayo kam tel'avel

Kiya lelakri me beshav".

Bring the three candles together. Take the rope or string and tie them to each other saying:

"As I tie this knot, I bind together .... (state your name and the name of your lover-to-be), in greatest love.

SO MOTE IT BE!"

After this snuff the candles out. The ritual is complete, and you can go about your normal business. Keep the tied candles in a safe place, away from people. This will act like a talisman and make your spell much more potent.

If after performing the above spell you get tired of the relationship that you have become involved in, then simply untie the knot and perform the incantation below.

Breaking the Bond

Acquire two white candles and a pink (or red) candle.

On the white candles inscribe your name and the name of your lover, on the pink candle inscribe the word "love". Hold these candles in your hands and visualize them becoming the thing they represent, i.e. the pink candle becomes filled with the power of love, and your candle becomes filled with your life energy, etc.

Now tie these candles together with a piece of red or pink rope, string or cord. Light the candles together. Say:

"Venti cinque carte siete!

Venti cinque diavoli diventerete,

Diventerete, Anderete

Nel'corpo, nel'sanquenell'anima,

Nell sentimenti del corpo;

Del mio amante non posso vivere,

Non passa stare nebere,

Ne mangiare ne . . . .

Ne con uomini ne con donne non passa Favellare

Finche ala pota dicasa mia

Non viene picchiare ! ".

18

Break the rope that binds the candles together. Now take the pink candle and blow it out, make sure that you don't blow out either the candle that represents you or the candle that represents your lover. Say:

"The bond is broken, and the light of love is dead!"

Now separate the other two candles and snuff them out. The spell is complete, and you should go about your normal affairs.

Very soon your partner will become restless and will feel that he/she wishes to end the relationship.

A Spell for Enhancing Passion

After performing the next rite, you will need fire extinguishers to calm the raging passion that will develop between you and your lover.

On a Friday, write on a plain piece of white or green paper, the name of the person you desire and your own name. Around this draw a heart.

Next you will need to obtain an apple. A green apple is best.

Cut the apple in half. Between the two halves place your piece of paper. Then hold the apple together with some string, cord or rope, and tie three knots in it. Then say:

"T're bact me ~av,

T're ba~t me piyav,

Dav tute m're ba~t

Kana tu mange sal".

Take a bite of the apple and eat it. At night go to your prospective lover's house and bury it in her/his garden. If the person does not have a garden, then bury it as near to her/his home as possible. If you can't bury it, hide amongst some bushes or trees.

You will notice the effects of this spell the next time you meet the person.

To Win Back a Lost Love

Many people find that they lose a lover to someone else, or the person leaves for reasons of his/her own, and this can be very damaging to your life. Worry no more, for here is a very powerful spell that will bring back any disenchanted lover.

For this spell you will need to obtain three leaves from a willow tree. The willow tree is held sacred by the Gypsies.

Go out to your garden. If you do not have a garden go to a park or into the countryside. Throw the leaves behind you one at a time. Each time saying:

"Per de, per de prajjina,

Varekaj hin hasz Kamav?

Basa, parro dz siuklo

Pirano dzal mai szigo".

Visualize your lover coming back to you each time you say this. The stronger the visualization the sooner the spell will manifest. It would also be a good idea to consecrate the talisman for Luck in Love. After drawing it out on parchment, prick yourself with a pin and let a few drops of blood fall onto it. Then hold up the talisman and say:

"Mro rat dav piraneszke,

Kasz Dikhav, Avava adaleske".

It should be noted that if parchment is unobtainable then only white paper should be used as a substitute.

Brenda Gets Her Man

Brenda, a shy 20-year-old, was employed in a Kiss-o-Gram agency as an office assistant. She was not very pretty and not at all outgoing. She felt destitute when she fell head over heels for a young model who started work in the Kiss-o-Gram agency. He never even noticed that she was alive.

Brenda came to us for help. We advised her to overcome her shyness and ask the man for a date. Believing in us, she complied.

Unfortunately, the results were devastating for her. The young man said no!

After discussing the matter, we felt rather guilty and decided to help Brenda with her love life. We gave her the spell for attracting a male. She was a little doubtful about its effectiveness, which was not surprising considering her lack of faith in us after our initial mistake, (we are only human, like everyone else).

She eventually agreed to try the spell and was not disappointed.

The next day at work the young man was being overly friendly and was spending more time in the office than he was out working.

Brenda knew the spell had started to work, so she prepared herself for the date, which she knew he would ask her for. She was right again. Two days later he asked her to go to lunch with him, and here he explained that he had made a terrible mistake refusing her date. They then began seeing each other regularly.

T.S.'s Lover

T.S. was having no luck with love, in fact he was having no luck with women. He found it hard to start a relationship and when he did it would turn out disastrous. The women he always dated were wrong for him. They would try to run his life, and this would lead him into the depths of despair.

Although he believed in the power of magic and mind power, he could never seem to make it work for him. By chance he stumbled upon the gypsy spell to attract a female. Although this spell was designed for a woman the magician already knows, he thought he would try it out with his own situation.

When performing the spell, he visualized women of all kinds being attracted to him, he saw them running towards him with open arms.

For three days nothing happened and T.S. was starting to doubt the spell. This was his mistake!

On the fourth day a few of his work mates asked him to go to a disco, he was reluctant. His past experience of discos and the women therein was not good. But after constant verbal attacks from his work mates he gave in.

That night T.S. couldn't believe his luck. All kinds of girls and women were coming straight up to him and asking for a dance. He also found it much easier to talk to these women, as he now felt a strange feeling of power over them.

This was by no means the end of it. From that day forth he has found it hard to go anywhere without getting a lot of attention from women.

Although he has not yet found his ideal partner at least he has plenty to choose from.

M.M. Breaks the Bond

M.M., an attractive 19-year-old girl, found that she was tiring of the relationship with her boyfriend of three years. She decided to rid herself of her boyfriend and free herself completely from his grip.

Her way to do this was through the gypsy spell. She put it to work immediately. The same day her lover came to her. He seemed restless and uptight. He started an argument and walked out.

Later that week he telephoned her to let her know it was all over and he no longer wished to have anything to do with her. Such is the power of magic.

Revenge

We know of one case where a magician used the "breaking the bond" spell to force two lovers apart. This magician became very jealous when an enemy of his started to date a very attractive blond-haired girl. This girl also happened to be close friends with the magician's girlfriend.

He decided to take action. He had no wish to perform a psychic attack for magical reasons - so he would break them up. This is exactly what he did. He used the gypsy way.

That same day the two lovers had a fierce argument and split-up on very bad terms.

Health-Curing Ailments

In the incantations that follow, you are calling on the aid of the "Pcuvuscheske", or earth spirit. In each of the incantations you are asking the "Pcuvuscheske" to take the illness from you and bring it into the earth. Here the earth neutralizes the illness and turns it from negative to positive energy.

So, while intoning the incantations it is important to visualize a cloud of blackness surrounding the affected part of your body.

While reciting the incantations see this blackness leaving your body via your feet. This will make it easier for the earth spirit to do his job.

A good idea to help your incantations along is to acquire a green candle to represent the "Pcuvuscheske". You may also use a white candle to represent you, if you wish. These candles are only an extra touch, they are by no means a necessity. If you choose to use them, then they will need to be consecrated.

Consecration

Take the candles and run them under the cold-water tap. Leave them to dry, do not dry them yourself. Once dried they should be inscribed with the appropriate name. The green one should be inscribed with the name "Pcuvuscheske" or "Earth Spirit". The white one should be inscribed with your name, or the name of the person to be healed.

These candles now symbolize the earth spirit and yourself, or, of course, the person to be healed.

Now to the incantations.

Stomach Pains

Hold your hand over your stomach, if right-handed use the right if left-handed use the left. The earth spirit will send healing energy through your hand, and into this area, as well as taking the illness from you. Say:

"Cuckerdya pal m're per

Caven save mise~e !

Cuckerdya pal m're per

den mise~eske drom odry prejial!"

Visualize the blackness moving down through your body to your feet, and out into the ground you stand on. The earth spirit will take care of the rest.

For Influenza

With this spell you will need to take parts of your body separately starting with your head. Then move to your upper half and then your lower half. Say:

"Shilalyi prejia,

pafiori me tut 'dav!

N afii me tut kamav;

Andakode prejia

odoy tut cuciden

odoy tut ferinen

odoy tut may kamen!

Mashurdalo sastyar !

Shilalyi, shilalyi prejia."

There will be an immediate improvement in your sleeping pattern. After about two days your sleepless nights should have disappeared forever, and the other symptoms of the "flu" will disappear with them.

With this spell the earth spirit will build up your natural resistance to the "flu" and the "cold". It will be a long time before you suffer again.

For Headache

This spell will take immediate effect. Remember to visualize the blackness around your head departing from your body through your feet. This spell is ideal for people who suffer from migraines. If the symptoms persist then we would strongly advise you to see a doctor, for this is a very effective spell. Stand up straight and relax your body. Take a deep breath and say:

"Oh duk andro m'ro shero

the o dad mise ;escro,

ada dikhel akana

man tu may dosta, mardyas,

miro shero tu mardyas !

Tu na ac tu andre me

ja tu, ja tu, ja kere.

Kay tu mise; cucides,

odoy, odoy sikoves !

Ko jal pro m'ro ushalyin,

adaleske e duk hin!"

For Sore Eyes

Hold both your hands over your eyes.
Visualize the blackness entering your hands
and going down to your feet. From here see
it leave your body and enter the ground
below.

mire muy na hin kere!

tut nikana me kamav,

Ac tu mange pal paca;

Kana e pcus yardakri

eveltele panori ! "

Money - A Constant Flow of Cash

For this spell you will need to use two silver coins. These can be of any value and size, but they must be silver. Take a clear bowl of water and to this add some table salt. This will then become cleaning fluid (spiritually and physically). Into this bowl place your coins. Say:

"You I cleanse as you grow and make me rich."

After two days take your coins out of the bowl. Go to the garden and dig a hole large enough to bury the coins in. If you do not have a garden, then you must bury them in a park or anywhere there is soil.

Once you have placed the coins in the hole pour some milk over them. The milk should be as fresh as possible. State your monetary desires. These can be anything from wanting the money for a new dress to wanting money for a brand-new car! Once you have stated your desires aloud, cover the hole. Try to hide it as much as possible, so no-one will dig it up. As people walk over this place your money worries will vanish and cash will start to flow to you regularly.

If you wish after six weeks you can dig up the coins and carry them with you at all times. But by that time, you should have no money problems and be quite satisfied with your financial situation, so you can leave them in the ground.

Material Objects

Here is a spell to acquire that long sought-after item, that previously you could never get your hands on. This spell is ideal for gaining an item that someone else will not give or sell.

Take an apple, a picture of the desired item (you can draw this yourself if you wish), and two leaves from a willow tree. Go to your garden and dig a hole large enough to hold all these items.

Place one of the willow leaves in the hole and state your desired object. Say:

"By the power of this willow, (state object) will be mine."

Take a bite of the apple, chew it and then swallow it. Say:

"By the power of this fruit, (state object) will be mine."

Place the apple in the hole on top of the willow leaf. Now hold the picture of your desired object and say:

"I call upon the Pcuvuscheske, grant me my wish."

Place the picture in the hole. On top of this place the other willow leaf. Say:

"Let my will be done, and not for the last time."

Fill in the hole and cover it well, so no-one will know that the ground has been tampered with. Within a short time, you will receive your desired object. Be open to all possibilities. You may receive it in a strange and unusual way.

Talismanic Wealth

The following talisman is ideal for bringing you material comforts of all kinds. When charging it keep in mind the type of wealth you want, or just think of all the good things in life as yours. It is fast and effective and should be carried with you at all times. If it is possible you should try to draw the talisman on parchment paper. If this is unavailable then draw it on plain white paper, with blue ink.

The talisman should be charged during the day. Try to charge it on a sunny day, as this is much more effective, for you are calling on the power of the sun God.

After drawing the talisman prick your finger with a needle and allow a few drops of blood to fall upon it. With both hands hold the talisman up towards the sun and mentally call on the power to enter the talisman through you. Feel the power running through your body and out your hands into the talisman before you. Call aloud the purpose of the talisman.

It is now charged, and you will not have to wait too long before you receive the wealth you seek. This wealth may start slowly at first, but don't let this put you off. The talisman will keep working for as long as it exists. It will constantly recharge itself. If you wish you can recharge it yourself every month with the same spell.

Money Magnet

This spell is designed so you can make yourself a money magnet. This magnet will attract money to you. Money is an energy and as energy flows, so you will be changing the direction of the flow, instead of more money going to the undeserving, a little bit will go to you.

For this spell you will need to use a silver coin of any value. Try to use one that is small, like a five pence piece, or twenty pence piece. As with the spell for constant cash, you will need a bowl of water into which you should put some salt. Wash the coin in this substance and dry it.

Now take a green candle and inscribe on it the letters "MMM".

Hold the candle and say:

"This candle will bring money to me from this day forth".

Now light the candle and let some wax fall on the coin. Quickly place the candle on top of the coin, so it is waxed there. You will need to keep an eye on the candle, as it burns, for it will not be totally stable because of the coin. This may cause the candle to fall and start a fire, so do be careful. Once the candle is stuck to the coin voice your monetary desires. Say:

"By the power of fire, by the vibrations of this candle, by the colour green, make me a magnet with the pull of the poles. As I will it, it is so. So, mote it be."

You have now constructed a money magnet. It will bring money to you often. With the above spells you will find that everything you touch seems to turn to gold, as you gain the Midas touch. Do not hoard your money. As we explained earlier, money is an energy. This energy should be allowed to flow through your life. By hoarding your wealth, you will stop the flow, and you could lose everything you gained. So, don't be afraid to spend money and enjoy yourself.

Each incarnation is too short to worry about finances. A very good idea is to take some of the money you gained through magic and give it to a charity. This is usually around ten per cent. Ecological groups are ideal to help, as they are trying to save this planet, we all live on, and it is the earth spirits you are receiving the magical help from with the above spells. After the successful outcome of your spells, give thanks. Take some fruit or milk and give it to the soil.

46

Dig a hole and put your offerings in it. This is great for the soil and it will please the earth spirits. This will make it much easier to gain their help again in the future.

Take your time with the spells, don't rush them. This may discourage the earth spirits from helping you. Treat the spirits with respect and they will do likewise. Remember you are much more superior than these creatures, so use your intelligence to your advantage.

Before ending the part of this book dealing with gypsy spells and incantations, we will give a gypsy talisman for second sight. The gypsies have been renowned through history for divinatory powers, and now you can be the same. Use their secret and see beyond normal vision.

Divination

Draw the talisman on parchment or, if unobtainable, ordinary white paper. Use black ink. Take the talisman in your hands and visualize a warm energy coming from it. Set it down and prick your finger with a needle. Allow a few drops of blood to fall on the paper. Now lift the talisman again. This time see a cool silver light all around it. Say:

"This talisman will give me second sight. It must be so".

Light a silver or white candle and place the talisman beside it.

Leave the candle to burn down. Once it has gone out, take the talisman and place it somewhere safe.

The first visions you start to receive may be confused. Don't try to strain too hard for explanations, these visions will clear with time, as you become accustomed to your new-found powers.

.Power Rites

These types of spells are used to enhance your own personal magnetism. They will help you to rise to the top of your chosen field. They can aid you in your business life by giving you a commanding aura.

Occultists have used spells like these to enhance their lives for centuries. You can also use them with the same effect.

Gaining Power Over Others

Take a white candle and on this inscribe your name. Cut an orange and place a small piece by your candle. You will need to rise at dawn on the first Sunday of any month. At this time light your candle and intone:

"As I consume this fruit,

I consume the power of Ra".

Leave the candle to burn down. This ritual will need to be repeated on the following two Sundays of the month. On the last Sunday of this month, the ritual changes slightly. Take two orange candles and hold them to the rising sun while you intone:

"Oh mighty Ra, vibrate these candles with your power".

Light the candles and beside these, place a fully peeled orange.

Lift the orange and say: ,

"With this I consume all that's thine, connect thine power with that of mine":

The spell is now complete, and you should leave the candles to burn down. The effects of this spell will become apparent immediately.

Personal Magnetism

Take a full orange and slice into it. Within this orange place a photograph of yourself.

Go to your garden or a park and dig a hole. In this hole place the orange. Sprinkle some cinnamon over the orange, and voice the following:

"Let me radiate like the sun's own rays. From this day forth, to the end of my days".

Once the ground accepts this offering, and the orange decomposes, your personal magnetism will be complete.

Revenge

There may come a time in your life when you feel the need to avenge yourself. We do not wish at this time to enter into the morality of Black Magic, this is for you to decide. If you feel that you are justified in performing one of these rites, then whatever we say will make no difference.

Revenge Spell

Acquire a photograph of your enemy; some salt, some suphur from an unburnt match. Scrape the red tip from match.

Throw some salt on the photograph. As you cast this salt intone:

"As this salt is of the earth,

so art thee.

And as I trod upon the earth,

so do I trod upon thee".

Now sprinkle the sulphur over the photograph, around the area of the forehead. Light the sulphur, so that it burns a hole in this region.

This will carry your incantation to the subconscious mind of your enemy, and he will therefore create his own downfall. Intone:

"Friends of fire, and friends of hell,

beckon to this horrid smell.

Destroy the empire that he's built,

let him suffer with his guilt.

From earth's own salt, and sulphur's smell,

With your own evil, you shall dwell.

With evil thought and vicious tongue,

I will undo what you have done.

No longer will you manipulate,

with your deeds you seal your fate.

The smell of vengeance is so sweet,

with these words my spell's complete".

Say the above with meaning, conjure up as much emotion as you can and keep in mind that whatever your enemy gets, he deserves!

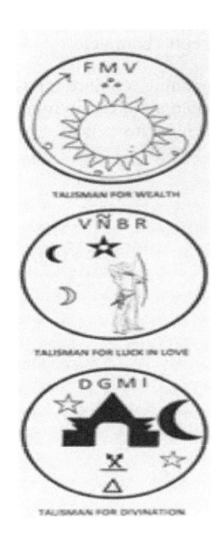

TALISMAN FOR WEALTH

TALISMAN FOR LUCK IN LOVE

TALISMAN FOR DIVINATION

56

The three talismans mentioned are here. Simply draw your own copy in accordance with the authors' instructions. Don't worry if you cannot do a good copy: the important thing is that you do it.

Made in the USA
Coppell, TX
05 April 2022